I0147310

Archibald Brown

The Danish Invasion of Cowal in the Tenth Century

An essay read before the Glasgow Cowal Society 30th January, 1874, with

additonal explanatory notes

Archibald Brown

The Danish Invasion of Cowal in the Tenth Century
An essay read before the Glasgow Cowal Society 30th January, 1874, with additonal explanatory notes

ISBN/EAN: 9783337183219

Printed in Europe, USA, Canada, Australia, Japan

Cover: Foto ©ninafisch / pixelio.de

More available books at **www.hansebooks.com**

THE

DANISH INVASION OF COWAL

IN THE

TENTH CENTURY:

AN ESSAY

READ BEFORE THE

GLASGOW COWAL SOCIETY

30TH JANUARY, 1874.

WITH

ADDITIONAL EXPLANATORY NOTES.

BY

ARCHIBALD BROWN,

MERCHANT, GREENOCK.

12 Brisbane St.

Greenock 19 June 187

This Essay is now printed at the special request of the GLASGOW COWAL SOCIETY, before whom it was originally delivered. The notes appended have chiefly been written since the Paper was read,--for details they require to be read in connection with the subjects referred to. The Author is sensible of his short-comings: but if he has in any measure been able to *spring a new mine in the old lore of his native district,* (a figurative compliment paid him by a member of the Society) his labour of love has its reward, and he will rejoice if the energetic members of the GLASGOW COWAL SOCIETY will spring other *mines,* as the *field* is far from being exhausted.

GREENOCK, *April, 1875.*

THE DANISH INVASION OF COWAL

TENTH CENTURY.

THE Danish invasion of Cowal in the Tenth Century is a subject much beset with difficulties : it being founded on circumstantial evidence handed down from that remote period, partly from the tradition of the district, and partly in old books and MSS.

The greatest difficulty to be encountered at the outset is to reconcile the different accounts given of this invasion. But, without further preface, I shall endeavour to make my Essay as intelligible as I can, by dividing it into three parts.

(1) In the first place I shall give an outline of the invasions of the Danes and Norwegians on the West Coast—from their first appearance in 793 A.D. till their invasion of Cowal in 918 A.D.

(2) Secondly, I shall endeavour to correct the mistaken notions about this invasion, viz.—the place of battle—the era in which it occurred—and the combatants engaged.

(3) And lastly, I shall show some of the evidences of the Danish invasion of Cowal in 918, and of their discomfiture there by King Constantine the Third, in the eighteenth year of his reign.(1)

In giving an outline of this invasion I shall mention some of the names by which these foreigners were known in the records of those times; and then give a summary of their

(1) Appendix A.

depredations on the West Coast of Scotland, and in Ireland,
prior to this battle. I presume it necessary to do so, as the
Danes and Norwegians were, and still are, often transposed
and confounded with each other in history. 2

Regarding their names, we find them called Nordmans or
Norwegians. Ostmen or Danes: also, Pagans, Gentiles, Vikingr,
&c. In the Irish annals they are called Galls or foreigners:
Genntih or heathens, and Lochlannaigh or Lakelanders. The
latter appellation, in its widest sense, included all the nations
north of the river Rhine. 3   But the depredations committed
on the West Coast were invariably confined to the Danes and
Scandinavians.   The Irish made a distinction between the
Danes and Norwegians.   The Danes, from their fair hair and
complexion, they called Fionnghaill: and the Norwegians,
from their dark hair and complexion, they termed Dubhghaill:
but both these foreigners are simply known in the tradition of
Cowal by the name Lochannaich.

The Dubhghaill or Norwegians, according to the ancient
histories of Ireland and Wales, seem to have preceded the
Danes upwards of fifty years.   Giraldus Cambrensis, in his
topography of Ireland, written about the middle of the twelfth
century, has five chapters on the depredations committed by
the Dubhghaill.   Dist. III. chap. 37 to 41.   He mentions
two of their distinguished leaders, namely, Gurmund and
Turgis.   Gerald is not very clear about the part played by
Gurmund, and others are sceptical of his existence; but Ussher
says that it was commonly believed by the Irish, that Gurmund
played a prominent part.   He further says:—Gurmund, and
after him Turgesius, notable pagans of Norway conquered and
ruled in Ireland in the ninth century of the Christian era.
" Gurmundi ac postea Turgesius Norwegensis principes pagani
in Hibernia debellata regnabant qui nono post Christian
seculo."   Ussher's Brit. Ecc. Primord. pp. 571-915.

In the Annals of Ulster British Museum, see Pinkerton's
Enquiry the early deeds of the Norwegians are thus recorded:—

(2) Appendix B.   (3) Appendix C.

793. The wasting of all the Islands of Britain by the Gentiles.
794. Burning of Reachrain by the Gentiles.
797. Spoils of the sea between Ireland and Scotland by the Gentiles.
801. Aoi of Columkille burnt by the Gentiles.
805. Sixty-eight of the family of Aoi were slain by the Gentiles."

The depredations of Gurmund seem thus to have been confined chiefly to the Western Islands ; but Turgis, his successor, in the first year of his career (815), invaded Ireland with a powerful fleet, and brought it into subjection. (Four Masters, p. 466 f. n.) Turgis afterwards resided at his fortress in Dublin, and at Dun Turgis in West Meath, and had his fleet stationed on the great lakes and estuaries throughout Ireland, from which he ravaged the adjacent territories. After thirty years of lawlessness he was waylaid and slain by the natives. (F. M. 467 f.n.)

About the time of Turgesius' death, the Fingalls or Danes made their first appearance in Ireland (845 to 848). The "Annals of the Four Masters" says. "In 847 A.D. a fleet of 140 ships of the King of the Gaill, or foreigners, came to Ireland to *attack the foreigners who were there before them*, so that between both they disturbed all Erin." (F. M. p. 468.) Their appearance seems to have created such a sensation in Ireland that their name "Fingallians" is the only record in the Annals of Ulster, (B. M.,) for the year 850.

According to Sir James Ware, they landed first at Dublin, and possessed themselves of the neighbouring country, which in his day was called Fingal. (Ware's Antiq., p. 59.)

The Dubhgalls or Norwegians who preceded them upwards of fifty years (already mentioned) took umbrage at the intrusion of their fair-haired brethren, and came to Dublin with a fleet of 140 ships, or as others have it 240 ships, and a bloody battle ensued, when the Danes of Dublin had the worst of it, and Dublin had been plundered by the victors. (Ware's Antiq.. pp. 58-59.) The Danes did not lose heart, for the

combat was renewed the following year, and the engagement
was so important, that it is the only event recorded in the
Annals of Ulster. B. M., for the year 851. " Battle between the
White Gentiles and Black Gentiles."

The editor of the Four Masters further says regarding this
engagement :—" About the years 850 and 851 the Norwegians,
with 160 ships, came to battle with the Danes at Snamh
Ednach or Carlingford Lough, and having fought with great
fury on both sides for three days and three nights, the Danes
were at length victorious, and the Norwegians at last were
obliged to leave their ships in their hands." F. M. p.648 f.n.

We thus learn, that, from 847 to 853, a period of six years,
these foreigners attacked each other with various successes,
and according to the Irish annals disturbed all Erin.

In the latter year of these conflicts, 853, according to Ware,
Aulaiv, Sitric and Ivar, three brothers, called Easterlings or
Danes, came in a great fleet and landed in Ireland, to whom
all the Danes in Ireland submitted, Ware's Antiq., p. 59.

Giraldus Cambrensis in other words says the same thing.
viz. :—" Not long after the death of Turgesius some adven-
turers, called Ostmen, arrived in Ireland. These foreigners
had for leaders three brothers, Amelaus, Sytaracus and
Yvorus." Dist. III., c. 43, p. 153.

Not only did the Danes of Ireland submit to these leaders
but the Annals of Ulster, B. M., shews that the submission had
been more general. It says—" In 853 Aulaiv, King of Lochlin,
came to Ireland, and *all* the *foreigners* of Ireland submitted
unto him, and he had rent from the *Irish.*" Thus shewing
that he and his brothers Sitric and Ivar had conquered the
whole inhabitants of Ireland. From this date, till the end of
this dynasty of Danish Kings, 4) which ceased about the year
948, we learn little or nothing of the doings of the Norwegians as a *ruling power* in Ireland or the Western Islands.

When these pirate kings got both foreigners and natives to
submit to them, Aulaiv took possession of Dublin, as the seat

(1) Appendix D.

of his power, Ivar of Limerick, and Sitric of Waterford; but Lochstrangford, which in the Annals of Ulster is called Lochdacaech, was their chief resort (5) when driven from Dublin in 902 and 917; but Dublin was the chief seat of their power, the mart of their plunder, and the scene of their dissensions. (Chal. Cal., Vol. I., p. 378 *f. n.*)

These Danish-Irish kings invaded other parts of Scotland on a large scale, on three different occasions, before they invaded Cowal in 918.

The Annals of Ulster (B. M.) says—"In 865 Aulaiv and his nobillitie went to Fortren, together with the foreigners of Ireland and Scotland, and spoiled the Cruithne or Picts, and brought their hostages with them."

869. "Aileluaith, was besieged by the Normans (Ostmen, Olaiv and Ivar; these two Norman Kings blockaded the place for four months, and at last destroyed it." (Johnston's Celto-Normanica.)

In the following year Olaiv and Ivar returned to Dublin, with 200 ships laden with booty; also, with many Anglorum, Britanorum, et Pictorum—that is, the Anglo-Saxons of West Lothian, the Britons of Strathclyde, and the Picts of Caledonia.

Their third expedition was made by Ivar O' Ivar, in the year 904. The Annals of Ulster says:—"Ivar O' Ivar, killed by the men of Fortren, with a great slaughter about him." Chalmers explains this event by saying:—"In the year 904 the Danes of Ireland, under Ivar O' Ivar, invaded North Britain on the west, and having penetrated into the country eastward with a view to the plunder of Forteviot, the Scottish capital, they were bravely encountered and their leader killed." (Cal., Vol. I., p. 384.)

This Ivar O' Ivar appears to have been the third son of Ivar the brother of Aulaiv. At his death he left three sons— Reginald, Sitric and Godfrey. They followed hard on the turbulent footsteps of their forefathers. A few years after the

(5) Appendix E.

death of their father we find them fighting among themselves at the Isle of Man. (Celto-Normanica.)

Reginald was obliged to maintain his authority by force, and, as would seem, desiring to possess North Britain as his progenitors possessed Ireland, formed a vast army, 'Pink. Enquiry, Vol. II., p. 182), and, according to Chalmers, conducted the Vikingr from Lochdaeaech to *the fatal shore of Lochfine in Cowal.* (Cal., Vol. I., p. 386 *f. n.*)

Having thus endeavoured to trace the movements of these foreigners, from their first appearance in 793 till their invasion of Cowal in 918, I come now to the second part of my Essay, and shall endeavour to correct the mistaken ideas about *the place of battle—the era in which it occurred—and the combatants engaged.*

This part of my Essay is rather an interruption to the thread of my subject ; but it is necessary to introduce it here, in order to clear away alleged objections to the Invasion of Cowal by the Danes in the Tenth Century.

I.—MISTAKE ABOUT THE PLACE OF BATTLE.

Till within a few years ago it was generally believed that this invasion was made from Ireland, on some spot about the banks of the Clyde. But the idea has now taken a new phase. Mr E. W. Robertson, author of the book called "Scotland under her Early Kings," published in Edinburgh in 1862), imagines that he has made the discovery that this battle had been fought, instead of at the Clyde, near the river Tyne in Yorkshire. As others have since too confidently followed this author, more particularly Dr Maclauchlan in his " Early Scottish Church," Edin., 1865, and Col. Robertson in his " Gael of Alban," Edin., 1866, it will be necessary to quote what Mr R. says on this point before showing the fallacy of his statement.

He begins by saying—In the year 917 — "Reginald, known by this time as king of the Dubhgalls, with his brother Godfrey, and the jarls Ottir and Gragaba, leaving the harbours of Waterford, sailed for the Northern shores of England, to assert the claims of the Dubhgall, as heir of his kinsman the Danish Halfden, to the fertile lands of Northumbria." In 918) " Landing amongst the kindred Danes of the North, Reginald marched at once upon York, seizing upon and portioning out amongst his followers and allies, the whole of the sacred patrimony of St. Cuthbert, with many a broad acre besides. Edred and his kinsmen, whose territories extended from the Tyne to the Forth, abandoning their dominions at the approach of the Norsemen, implored the aid of the Scottish Constantine to stem the torrent of invasion. In Constantine they found a prompt ally, and strengthened by the support of the Scottish army, the Northumbrian leaders prepared with renewed courage to march against the foe. The hostile armies met on the moor near Corbridge, on Tyne, where Reginald, who had decided upon awaiting the attack of the confederates, holding his immediate followers in reserve in a position where they were concealed from the assailants, he ranged the main body of his army in three divisions, under the command respectively of his brother Godfrey, the two jarls, and the chieftains, to whom the Irish give the title of 'the young leaders.' So impetuous was the onset of the Scots and Northumbrians that at the first shock the Norsemen were overthrown. the heaviest loss falling on the followers of the jarls, a contingency which Reginald had probably calculated, as they bore the brunt of the battle. Animated at their success, and anxious to improve their advantages, the allies pursued eagerly onwards regardless of the enemy's reserve. which Reginald now poured upon the flank and rear of the victors—disordered in the confusion of pursuit—inflicting in his turn severe loss, and restoring the fortune of the day. Edred was slain in the final struggle with many of his Northumbrian followers, who appear to have suffered most severely, until the approach of night separated the combatants, and put a stop to a contest which led to no decisive result." (E. W. Robertson's " Scotland under her Early Kings," Vol. I. pp. 37-59.)

The authorities given by Mr R. for the above glowing description of the battle are Simeon of Durham's Life of Saint Cuthbert, the Pictish Chronicle, the Saxon Chronicle, and the Annals of Ulster. Having examined copies of said authorities I have to say, that none of them, nor the whole put together, will bear Mr R. out in his statements. Taking these old annalists in the above order, I shall allow them to speak for themselves. Simeon of Durham says:— " During the period when Edward was governor of the kingdom, (910-915), not only of the Western Saxons, but of the Eastern Angles and Northumbrians, a certain pagan king named Reingwold landed on the Northumbrian shore with a large fleet, without any delay he broke in upon York, and either killed or drove out of the country the most influential of the inhabitants." (The Historical Works of Simeon of Durham, Translated from the Original by the Rev Jos. Stevenson. London, 1856. Chap. xxxi., p. 667.)

The Pictish Chronicle, a document of the tenth century, and transcribed at York in the fourteenth century, says:—" In the 18th year of Constantine the Third the battle of Tinmore was fought between Constantine and Regnall, and the Scots were victorious."

Bellum Tinmore, factum est in XVIII anno inter Constantinum et Regnall, et Scotti habuerant victoriam.

The Saxon Chronicle says :—" In the year 923 Regnold took Eboraci or York by force."   Anno DCCCCXXIII Hoc anno Regnoldus rex expugnavit Eboracum.

And the Annals of Ulster (in B. M. see Pinkerton's Enquiry runs thus :—" The Gentiles of Lochdacaech left Ireland and went for Scotland—the men of Scotland, with the assistance of the Northern Saxons, prepared before them. The Gentiles divided themselves into four battles (or battalions), viz., one by Godfrey O' Ivar, another by the two earls, the third by the young lords, and the fourth by Rannall Mac Biolach, who lay in ambush, that the Scots did not see ; but the Scots overthrew them they saw ; that they had a great slaughter of them about Ottir and Gragava; but Rannall gave the onset behind the Scots, that he had the killing of many of them, only that neither king nor murmor was lost in the conflict. The night discharged the battle."

You will observe that Simeon of Durham never refers to King Constantine and the Scots being engaged at York against Reingwold the pagan, neither does the Saxon Chronicle; therefore, so far as Scotland is concerned, their evidence goes for nothing.

On the other hand, the Pictish Chronicle states that it was a battle between Constantine and Regnall, and that the Scots were victorious. I may remark, if the alleged war was undertaken in behalf of the Saxons, how was their name, and also the death of King Edred, ignored in this chronicle The Annals of Ulster, as we have already seen, says distinctly that neither king nor murmor (maormor) was slain.

But some might be ready to ask, how were the Northern Saxons the allies of the Scots on this occasion? The answer is easily given. It was not necessary to go to York for the Saxons' assistance, as the Saxons, since the year 547, were in possession of the Lothians, *(which in old charters were called Saxonia.)* Their territories reached as far west as the river Esk, while the Angles possessed settlements beyond that river along the south side of the Forth as far as Abercorn. (Skene's Chron., Pref., p. 79.)

From this we see that the Scots and Saxons were living contiguous to one another, on both sides of the river Forth, consequently, nothing would be more natural than that they should make common cause against their mutual enemies—the Danes and Norwegians.

But apart from Mr E. W. Robertson and his followers, all antiquarians of any note who have treated of this subject, shew that the invasion in 918 was made on the West of Scotland.

Chalmers, in his Caledonia, says—"The invasion was made from Ireland by the Danes under Reginald, who directed his fleet into the Clyde." (Vol. I., p. 385.)

Skene, in his Preface to the Scots and Picts Chron., echoes what the Pictish Chronicle and Annals of Ulster records on this event.

Pinkerton in his " Enquiry" says " The Norwegians and Danes of Ireland formed a vast army, and landed in North Britain." (Vol. II., p. 182.)

The " Four Masters " says—" The Galls went from Lochdacaech to Alba, and Constantine the son of Aedh gave them battle."

J. J. A. Worsaae, in his book " The Danes and Norwegians in Scotland," says—In the beginning of the tenth century the Scotch king Constantine the Third, in conjunction with the more northern Anglo-Saxons, beat the Danes who had passed over from Dublin under Reginald and Godfrey O' Ivar, in a great battle *near the Clyde.* See. IV., p. 180, London, 1852.

In short, Robertson's plausible story seems to have been founded on *two names—Reginald* and *Tinmore.* Regarding the first he infers, that because a certain Reingwold made some depredations at York, between the years 910 and 923, the same must be Reginald the Danish-Irish king, who invaded Scotland in 918. I may observe, in passing that Reginald was a common name among the Danes about this era. Chalmers says—" Among the Danish reguli of Ireland and Northumberland the same name occurs so frequently, that different persons are often confounded." Cal., Vol. I., p. 388 *l. u.* And certainly we have a case in point. As regards Tinmore, the only authority for this name is the Pictish Chronicle (6); but that document does not say where that place was, nor am I aware, that any author who has copied from that Chronicle with the exception of Mr Robertson and his followers, has condescended to fix its locality.

II. - MISTAKE ABOUT THE DATE OF THE BATTLE.

The second mistake, which I shall briefly notice, is the *date fixed on the* (recent) *Government Survey Map of these*

(6) Appendix F.

memorable engagements. I think I can easily conceive how the surveyors have dated these battles the *eleventh* instead of the *tenth* century.

Having had some conversation on this subject with Mr Lyon, R.E., the head of the Surveying Department in that locality in 1863, I clearly understood that he placed much reliance on the account supplied in 1790-1 by the Rev. John M'Kinnon, Parish Minister of Kilmodan, to Sir John Sinclair, for his ecclesiastical statistics. I have no doubt that Mr Lyon recommended it to his superiors, and that it had been adopted accordingly.

Mr M'Kinnon's statement on this subject is as follows:—
" The most ancient name of this parish is Gleann-du-uisg, signifying the glen of black water. Afterwards a battle was fought between Meckan, the son of Magnus, King of Norway, and the Albuins or Gail, when, it was said, the Norwegians were slaughtered on each side of the river Ruail, which runs through the middle of the glen : and their bodies being thrown into the river, gave the colour of blood to it. Hence the parish got the name of Glendaruel, and the river the name of Ruail, which signifies the Glen-of-red-blood."

With *two* exceptions, the above description is exactly still the tradition in the locality. These exceptions are the *names Meckan* and *Norwegians.* The Norwegians are not known by that name to the natives of Cowal. The only name by which the northern invaders are known, whether Danes or Norwegians, is by that of Lochannaich, which means either, and as to Magnus, King of Norway, on whose name *really* hangs this date, he is well known in history, having subdued the Orkney Islands about the end of the eleventh century (Cal. Vol. I., p. 342) ; also, the Hebrides, and made some plundering expeditions to Ireland, (Cal., Vol. I., pp. 615-616) : but, that he invaded the mainland of Argyleshire is without any foundation — not even Kintyre — it is alleged he had secured that by treaty from Malcolm Canmore, in the following manner, that all the islands he could sail round about

were to be his own, and in order to include the peninsula
of Kintyre with the rest of the islands, he caused his galley
to be dragged across at Tarbert, while he sat at the helm.
Chalmers, one of our best historians, says regarding this affair,
"The tale is altogether unworthy of any writer who regards
fact more than fiction."   Cal., Vol. I., p. 605 f. n.

As to Meckan the son of Magnus, who is thus immortalised in
the history of Cowal, my humble opinion is, that there was never
such a person, and I shall give you my reason for thinking so :
firstly, that his name never appears in any document prior to
the Rev. Mr M'Kinnon's ; and secondly, (properly speaking',
his name cannot be said to exist in the traditions of the
locality.

That a northern invader was buried where Meckan's *rude*
grave is marked on the map, I believe ; but that his name
was Meckan, I do not believe.   The name Meckan bears on
the face of it to be nothing else than a topographical blunder
—tradition having rendered a common into a proper noun.

The name of the place is spoken under two forms in the
Gaelic language, viz., Uamh-bhar-a-Mheacain, and Rudha-
bhar-a-Mheacain.   Bar-a-Mheacain is a name made up of two
Gaelic words—*bar*, the top of a conical hill or any eminence,
and *meacan*, the root of a tree or that of an esculent plant.
When associated with that grave it is called Uamh or Uaigh-
bhar-a-Mheacain, or the grave on the conical hill or promontory abounding with roots.   This is literally the case at the
present day ; around the site of the grave the roots of the
trees are beautifully interlaced over the surface of the rocks.
Such topographical errors are not uncommon around that
locality.   Lochruel, which derived its name from the famous
battle in question, is printed on the Government Charts Loch-
riddan—a silly name, being neither Gaelic or English.   And
again, we have Ellangreg, Allangreg and Ealan-Gheirig,(7) a
place famous in history.   The real name of the island is
Eilean-dearg or red island in contra-distinction to the black

(7) Appendix G.

isle of Caladh on the opposite side of the loch ; but the name of the island of old being associated with its castle, was called Caisteal-an-Eilean-dheirg, or the castle of the red island. Eilean-dheirg was stupidly converted into Ellangreg. I have no doubt but Meekan's name was produced in the same way—hence the mistake of founding the date of the battles on his name.

III. MISTAKE IN SUBSTITUTING PERSONS FOR PLACES.

The third and grand mistake, and that in which antiquarians have generally erred, is in their supposing that the battlefields in Cowal derived their names from some of the *leaders* of this invasion.

I shall here again refer to the order of battle. The Annals of Ulster (in B. M.) says :—" The Gentiles divided themselves into four battles (or battalions) viz., one by Godfrey O' Ivar, another by two earls, the third by the young lords, and the fourth by Rannall Mac Biolach (who lay in ambuscade), that the Scots did not see ; but the Scots overthrew the three (battalions) they saw, that they had a great slaughter of them *round Ottir and Gragava*." Some antiquarians have supposed that the above nameless earls or jarls must have been called Ottir and Gragava, consequently they have called them so,(8) rendering this link of history a perfect enigma.

It is true that Mr W. F. Skene, in his collated copy of the Annals of Ulster, has the names of Otter and Gragabai introduced into the text. His version begins thus, " The Galls of Lochdacaech expelled from Erin, viz., Ranald, King of the Dubhgalls, and the two earls Ottir and Gragabai," &c. This explanation evidently has been foisted into the text, and that by a late scribe, who did not understand the subject, as I shall briefly shew. *Firstly*, the Galls were not expelled from Erin, but deliberately prepared to invade Scotland, and that on a large scale. Mr Skene's version farther on shows this. For, we are informed, that the men of Alban, with the

(8) Appendix II.

assistance of the Northern Saxons, had time to make a corresponding preparation to resist them, having come across the
country and met them at their landing place. *Secondly*, Reginald, by nation was a Fingall or Dane, and *not* a Dubhgall or
Norwegian, and since the accession of his dynasty to power
in 853, the Dubhgalls were united with, but subjects to, the
Fingals. From the days of Duald M'Firbis, who made the
Norwegians Fiongalls and the Danes Dubhgalls (like Sir
Walter Scott's mistake about Maccallnmmore too many of our
historians, including Mr Skene, unwittingly put white in place
of black. (See Appendix B.)

Let us look more narrowly into the terms Ottir and Gragava.
Mr Skene, in his copy of the Annals of Ulster, gives the para-
graph in Irish Gaelic, which reads thus :—" Roinis re feraib
Alban fors na tri catha ad concadar corolsat ar n-dimar do na
Genntib im Ottir acus im Graggabai." This sentence is translated by Mr Skene, " The three battalions which they saw were
routed by the men of Alban, and there was a great slaughter
of the Gentiles, round Otter and Gragabai." I have submitted
this passage to a competent Irish scholar, who has no doubt
whatever that " im Ottir acus im Gragabai" were intended for
places and not for persons. Admitting this, we have a simple
key that opens the door to solve this tangled problem.

I shall endeavour to show you immediately that the Ottir
and Gragabai referred to are none else than the district of
Otter on Lochfineside ; and the farm of Garvie or Garbh-
amhain in Glendaruel the places where the men of Alban
encountered the Danes. Oitir is variously spelled Oitir,
Ottir and Ottar ; whereas Garvie or Garbh-amhain, a rough or
rocky river, is spelled Gragava, Cracava, Gragabai, Gragabau,
&c., both of which are imitations of the sound.

THE TRADITIONARY EVIDENCE OF THE DANISH INVASION OF COWAL.

Having disposed of the objections that are alleged against the Danish Invasion of Cowal in the Tenth Century, I shall now, in the last place, introduce the internal evidence of those battles, and show how exactly it agrees with the written records of that period.

The Danish invaders, on leaving Lochdacaech, formed their fleet into four divisions: Godfrey, the brother of Reginald, led the van, followed respectively, by the divisions of the jarls and chieftains, while Reginald himself brought up the rear or reserve, and conducted the expedition to the fatal shore of Lochfine in Cowal. (Cal., Vol. I., p. 386 *f. n.*)

It appears that Constantine was well aware where the invaders intended to land, for the Annals of Ulster says :—" The men of Albun, with the assistance of the Northern Saxons, *prepared before them.*" The most direct way for Constantine and his allies to march against the foe, was through Menteith and Lennox towards the upper parts of Cowal, and onward into Glendaruel. This line of march had its difficulties, but it also had its safeguards. Constantine was well aware of the superiority of the Danish fleet over his own, (if he had any), and it was his wisdom to avoid it ; and he knew also if he and his allies were defeated they could fall back on their natural defiles, where the enemy could not follow them with impunity. Constantine appears to have fixed his head quarters at Garvie, and pushed the main body of his army to meet the foe at his landing place at Oitir.

The first three divisions of the invading army landed at Oitir, but it appears that Reginald, though he conducted them " to the fatal shore of Lochfine in Cowal," did not land his division there. Seeing the hostile army of the Scots making their appearance on the heights of Oitir, he made a diversion in order to attack the allies in flank and rear, by sailing

backward round Rudha-na-h'airde or Ardlamont Point, and
into Lochruel. Having reached there, he moored his gallies at
the head of the loch, landed his army, and marched it to the
narrow neck of Glendaruel, south of " Bealach-an-droighinn"
bridge, known to this day as " Srath-nan-Lochannach," or the
Field of the Danes. The position chosen agrees exactly
with what the Annals of Ulster says :—"A battalion under
Ranall in ambuscade, which, however, the men of Alban did
not see." From this place of concealment he could pounce on
either the flank or rear of the Scots army.

The other three battalions, on landing at Oitir, separated
into two divisions, and aimed at crossing the hill at each end
of the district. The division at its upper part made its way
into Glendaruel—then called Gleann-du-uisg—evidently with
the intention of cutting off king Constantine and his reserve
from the main body of the allied army ; but in this they were
disappointed, being bravely encountered by Constantine and
his retainers. The old Ecclesiastical Statistics says :—" The
Lochannaich were slaughtered on each side of the river which
runs through the middle of the glen, and their bodies being
thrown into the river, gave the colour of blood to it; hence
the parish got the name Glendaruel (or as in old documents
Glenrowel), and the river and loch the qualifying adjective
Ruel or Ruadhfhuil, red blood." (9.

The other section of the Danish army, which aimed to cross
the hill at the southern end of the district above Kilfinan,
met the main body of the Scots army near the top of the hill,
in a place called Gleann-a-chatha. In the " Origines Parochialis
Scotiae," of 1534 and 1541, it is respectively spelled " Glenchow,"
and " Glencaw." A large field or slope in this Glen is called
Acha-ghlinn-a-chatha, literally, The-Field-of-the-Glen-of-the-
Battle. It appears it was there the brunt of the battle took
place, (10) and " when routed by the men of Alban," the battle
became desultory over the whole district, as the numerous
cairns, &c., indicate. (11)

(9) Appendix I.   (10) Appendix J.   (11) Appendix K.

While a simultaneous battle was going on at Oitir and Garvie, (according to the Annals of Ulster,) " Reginald, who lay in ambush at Srath-nan-Lochannach, made an attack on the men of Alban from behind, and slew many of them, but neither their king, nor any maormor fell by him."

His position could not be seen either in Oitir or at Garvie, and from his place of concealment, he could fall upon the flank and rear of the Albanich.

His attack from behind would most likely be made upon Constantine's reserve, which would pursue the fugitives over the hills from Glendaruel to their ships. No sooner did Constantine discover Reginald's ambuscade, than he concentrated his army against him, and drove him back to his encampment at Srath-nan-Lochannach. There Reginald made a determined stand, and a severe struggle took place. The situation is yet called Caigean-na-cruadail, or the conflict of valour ; and close beside the Caigean there is a ford on the river, called Ath-nan-claigean, or the ford of sculls. (12.) Reginald soon found out that his single battalion could not cope with Constantine's elated army, therefore he beat a hasty retreat to his gallies. Constantine pursued him to Lochruelhead, where he rested his army at Rudha-bhar-a-mheacain, also called Creag-na-h-anaileach, or the rock of resting. The Pictish Chronicle well might say, " This battle was fought between Constantine and Regnall, and the Scots were victorious." Reginald then collected his shattered army, and returned to Ireland, where it appears the result of the expedition was anything but satisfactory to his followers. It is recorded in the Annals of Ulster, that he was slain two or three years afterwards. 920 or 921, " Reginald O' Ivar, King of Dubhgalls and Fiongalls killed," (Celto-Normanica.)

In conclusion, I may, without ostentation say, that it is both a pride and satisfaction to the natives of Cowal to think (13) that the resistance which the impregnable fortress of Dumbarton could not make, the Danes found among the hills and

(12) Appendix L.   (13) Appendix M.

D

glens of Cowal. So scared were they with the warm reception they met, that this Danish dynasty, though for many years afterwards doing much mischief in Ireland, did not venture to invade the west of Scotland on a large scale ever afterwards.

APPENDICES.

APPENDICES.

APPENDIX A.

The name Constantine was in use among the Picts previous to their union with the Scots of Dalriada. No doubt they borrowed it from a foreign source. The following various ways of spelling Constantine, and of his father Hugh's name, give an idea of how proper names were spelled in early times :—

Orig. Date.	Documents.	Names.
995 A.D.	Pictish Chron.	Constantinius filius Edu
1014-1022 „	Flann Mainistreach.	Constantin mac Aeda.
1065 „	Chron. of the Scots.	Constantinus fil. Hed.
1070 „	Duan Albanach.	Cusantin mac Aodh
1140-1172 „	Hist. Britonum.	Custantin fil. Aeda.
1167 „	Chron. Scots and Picts.	Constantine Mak Edha.
1215 „	Ann. of Innisfallen.	Cansantin.
1251 „	Chron. of Scots and Picts.	Constantine, Mack Ethn.
1270 „	Chron. Elegieam.	Constantine fil. Ethaide.
1280 „	Chron. Picts and Scots.	Constantine mac Edha.
1290 „	Chron. of Huntingdon.	Constantinus fil. Hed.
1317 „	Chron. of Picts and Scots.	Caustantin fil. Edha.
1334 „	Chron. of the Scots.	Constantinus fil. Ath.
1348 „	Chron. of the Scots.	Constantius fil Aeth.
———	Chron. Rhythmicum.	Constantinus fil. Ed.
1498 „	Annals of Ulster.	Custantin mac Aeda.

APPENDIX B.

The commencement of the confusion, about the appearance of the Danes and Norwegians, can be traced to the Irish seanachies of the seventeenth century. The editor of the "Annals of the Four Masters," says—" A distinction was made by the Irish between the Danes and Norwegians from the colour of their hair and complexion. The Danes, according to Duald Mac Firbis and others, being denominated Dubh-Lochlannaigh, signifying Black-lake-landers, being chiefly dark-haired ; and the Nor-wegians, Fionn-Lochlannaigh, or White-lake-landers, being mostly of a fair complexion, with fair or reddish hair. (F. M., 460 f.n.) Mac Firbis, shortly before his death (he was killed in 1670, *Ibid.*) had been employed by Sir James Ware, in collecting and translating Irish MSS. This ac-

counts for Sir James propagating this mistake, who says on this point
" Some divide the men of the North and East into Normans and Ostmen,
Dubhgalls and Fionngalls. The Dubhgalls, or black foreigners, meaning
the Danes, and the Fionngalls, or white foreigners, the Norwegians."
(Ware's Antiq. of Ireland, Chap. VI. p. 19.)

The seanachies' mistakes have been perpetuated by such eminent historians as Mr W. F. Skene, in his " History of the Highlanders," and by
Browne, in his " Highland Clans." Pinkerton, on the other hand, reverses
this idea, but accounts for the distinction in a new way. He says—
" In the old Irish writers, as "Tighernac," and the " Annals of Ulster,"
&c., Fingal, or white strangers, is a name uniformly given to the Danes,
as Dugal, or black strangers, is the peculiar name of the Norwegians." He
gives the cause of the distinction by saying— " Mr Thorkelin, a learned
native of Iceland, informs me that the old dress of the Norwegians, and
especially of the pirates and mariners, was black, as the Icelanders is at
this day, and has always been." (Enq., vol. II., p. 74.) The new idea
about the black dress has been adopted by Donald Gregory, in his " Western Highlands and Islands," and by Robertson, in his " Scotland under
her Early Kings." It is surprising that it did not occur to Pinkerton and
his followers, that the doings of the Dugals and Fingals were a matter of
history in Ireland, many years before Iceland had been inhabited. We
learn that Iceland had only been discovered about the year 860, and
colonised in the year 874. (M'Kenzie's Travels in Iceland, Edin. 1811.)
The Northmen, or Norwegians mentioned in the Irish Annals, from 795 to
847, are invariably termed Galls and Gentib, but, from the arrival of the
Danes, or Fingals, about the latter date, till about the year 920, the two
nations were distinguished by the terms Dubhgalls or Norwegians, Fionngalls or Danes. This distinction seems to have been given up about the
latter date, as the term Gall is simply used, and in later times Dugal and
Fingal were adopted as proper names.

But descending to our own times, it is patent to all who have visited
Norway, that the genuine natives of that country along the sea-coast,
from the Nase to Lapland, are as swarthy and dark-haired as the natives
of the West of Scotland, but, on the other hand, along the shores of Denmark and Sweden, the inhabitants invariably have fair or reddish hair,
with sallow or florid complexion. This distinction does not arise from a
difference of RACE, as many foolishly imagine, but from natural causes,
which can easily be accounted for, viz.,— From *Soil*, *Climate*, and the effects
of the *Gulf Stream*. It is a well known fact that the great body of tepid
water, called the Gulf Stream, flows from the tropics northwards, past the
west of Britain and Ireland, and along the coast of Norway, keeping all
the lochs and fiords free of ice during winter. The warm vapours arising
out of it are either attracted by the mountains, or driven towards them.

by the south and west winds, which prevail during the greater part of the year. The air on the land being much colder than that on the sea, particularly during the fall of the year, causes the vapours to descend in superabundance of rain, so as to darken the air, and charge the soil like a soaked sponge. The late Dr Livingstone observes that warm moisture even darkens the colour of Africans. He says—" Heat alone does not cause blackness, but heat and moisture combined do materially darken the colour. Wherever we find people who have lived for *ages in a humid district*, they are deep black." (Travels in Africa, Chap. XVIII., p. 338. London, 1857.)

On the other hand, the effect of the Gulf Stream is not felt in Denmark. It never enters the German Ocean nor the Baltic Sea. During winter the Baltic Sea is frozen up, and also the bays and rivers south of it, on the coast of Denmark. The rainfall in summer is much less there than on the coast of Norway, and what does fall, is instantly absorbed by the sandy soil, which prevails everywhere.

We thus see that the Norwegians, or Dubhgalls, dwell in a damp climate, and, that the Danes in one the reverse of that. The soil of Denmark, being sandy, imparts its sallow tinge to the complexion of the inhabitants. The bleaching effects of the sun on the human hair is well known. We often see in this country, the hair of children and even adults, who go about bare-headed in summer, getting like half-bleached flax, and remaining so until the duskiness of winter restores it to its wonted colour, or rather imparts to it a deeper shade. But this bleaching process of the hair goes on all the year round in Denmark. The dry summers and frosty winters of that country do not effect a corresponding change on the hair and complexion as on the west coast, which is subject to the effects of the Gulf Stream. The same remarks are applicable to the distinction of Tacitus, which has been retailed threadbare, viz., That the fair or red hair of the Caledonians betokened a German extraction, while the dark hair and complexion of the Silures indicated a Spanish origin. The same natural causes, to a certain extent, operated on the appearance of the Caledonians and Silures, which they did on the Fingalls and Dubhgalls. The Silures, who inhabited the mountains of South Wales, were subject to the darkening effects of the Gulf Stream, whereas the Caledonians, with whom Agricola came in contact, were situated along the German Ocean, where the Gulf Stream is not felt. The climate there being comparatively dry, and the soil being generally sandy, or of red clay, gave its tinge of colour to the hair and complexion of the inhabitants. In a word, there is no proof whatever that the Germans found a footing on the East of Scotland, where, Tacitus says, there is a resemblance between them and the Caledonians. But, on the other hand, we have positive proof that the Hebrides were occupied and ruled by the Norwegians for upwards of four hundred years (793 to 1263) where they have left many traces of their race and language. If the Norwegians were the fair-haired, light complexioned people alleged, there would be more traces of their appearance and prowess in the Western Islands than anywhere else in Scotland. But strange to say, our would-be philosophers find there only the last wave of the Celtic race—the degenerate, swarthy, black-haired Gael, pure and simple.

What an amount of sheer nonsense and vicious deductions have resulted from the writings on *Races* by such men as Pinkerton and M'Culloch—idle speculations which were recently adopted as ascertained facts, by Johnston in his Physical Geography.

APPENDIX C.

In a Gaelic MS. of the Eighth or Ninth Century, entitled, "SLOGHA CHEASAIR AN INIS BHREATAN," the southern boundary of Lochlan is given as follows : —" Ceasar-thainig go leigionibh lan iomdhaidh do ogaibh ainseire na Headail leis an garbh fhearan na Gallia agus tire leathan fhada Lochlain. Ar is aoin tir iadsan acht edarchuigheacht sroth Rein roghlain ag dlutha agus ag dealughadh na da fhearan sin." Which means in English— " Ceasar came with some entire legions of the ruthless youths of Italy into the rough land of Gaul, and the wide and long country of Lochlain. For these are one and the same country, but, for the interposition of the clear current of the Rhine, which divides and sunders the two lands." (H. S. Rep on Ossian's Poems, p. 309.)

APPENDIX D.

The following is a chronological table of the Danish reguli in Ireland, during the period of their expeditions to North Britain—

Anlaiv and Ivar his brother, ruled from	-	-	853-872 A.D.
Ostin the son of Anlaiv	„ -	-	872-875 „
Godfred the son of Ivar,	.. -	-	875-888 „
Sytrig the son of Ivar, governed alone,	-	-	888-892 „
Sytrig and Godfred Merle, jointly ruled,	-	-	892-896 „
Ivar, the son of Ivar, governed from	-	-	896-904 ..
Reginald, the son of Ivar, ruled.	-	-	904-921 „
Godfrey, the son of Ivar, governed,	-	-	921-934 „
Anlaiv, the son of Godfrey, ruled.	-	-	934-941 „
Blackar, the son of Godfrey, ruled,	-	-	941-948 „
Godfrey, the son of Sitrig, -	-	-	948- „

(See Chal. Cal., Vol. I., pp. 378-379 f.n.)

APPENDIX E.

The "Annals of the Four Masters," Dr Reeve, Mr Skene, and others, place Lochdacaech at Waterford, but Chalmers affirms it to be Lochstrangford. I do not pretend to say which is right, but for several reasons would be inclined to think that Lochstrangford is the place meant, it being situated in the centre of their depredations. From its shallowness, it was admirably suited for their gallies—the entrance to it being narrow, was easily defended—within its basin they had spacious and safe accommodation; and in every respect it was an excellent harbour of refuge. Waterford, on the other hand, was far from the centre of their depredations, though one of their first settlements.

APPENDIX F.

The Pictish Chronicle, according to Mr Skene, is really the chronicle of the monks of Brechin, and was compiled between the years 977 and 995, and the copy published, was transcribed at the see of York, in the 14th century. It might be suspected that the transcriber could have fallen into the same mistake as the author of " Scotland under her Early Kings " did about Timmore. The transcriber being an ecclesiastic of the see of York, local affairs with similar names might bulk in his mind, and mix up in the summary he gives, with events of greater moment. Mr Skene says, regarding this production—" This MS. is of the fourteenth century, and has evidently been transcribed at York, by Robert de Populton, as there appears at fo. 221, 'ora pro Popilton qui me compilavit Eboraci,' and again at fo. 213 and 262, 'ora pro fratre Roberto de Populton.' Mr Skene further observes, ' Populton appears to have transcribed it from another MS. and not always correctly.

APPENDIX G.

Any remarks about this island or its Castle, are foreign to the subject of this essay, yet a short note about them may not be unacceptable to my Cowal readers.

The Campbells of Eilean Dearg, who preceded the present Campbells of Southhall in the lower part of their estate, are celebrated in history and Gaelic song. But I pass over their fame, and confine my remarks to the eventful history of this island in 1685. Under the walls of its castle the Earl of Argyle stationed his fleet, and made the last stand when he unsuccessfully invaded the kingdom in that year.

The story may be thus told—In 1681 the Jacobite nobles became jealous of the great possessions and powerful influence of the Earl of Argyle,

E

and James, Duke of Albany and York, who virtually ruled the kingdom then, being a bigoted papist, cordially hated him for his Protestant leanings.

He was therefore conspired against, and a plot laid to entrap him about taking the Test or oath of allegiance. After some scheming, he was seized and confined, and after a mock trial, was convicted of treason ; but, while awaiting the sentence of death from London, he escaped from his confinement in the Castle of Edinburgh, in the garb of a page, holding up the train of Lady Sophia Lindsay, his step daughter. After many narrow escapes, he fled to London, and afterwards to Holland.

The Scottish exiles in Holland met at Amsterdam on 17th April, 1685, when it was resolved to invade Scotland, and to make war against James the Seventh. They unanimously elected Archibald Earl of Argyle, to be their captain-general.

On the first of May, the Earl and his followers sailed from the river Vhli, in three ships laden with arms and ammunition, but having on board less than three hundred men, all told.

The voyage at first promised well. Within a week they arrived at the Orkney Islands. Being in need of a pilot, Argyle, very unwisely, allowed two of his principal men to land, who were seized at once by the Bishop of Kirkwall. As a reprisal, the Earl seized a few persons, and sailed down the West Coast of Scotland.

Having arrived in the Sound of Mull, he sent his son Charles ashore among his friends and former retainers, but to little purpose. Burnet gives the reason of his failure as follows :- " Argyle found that the early notice the Council had of his designs, had spoiled his whole scheme. For they brought (almost) all the gentlemen of his country to Edinburgh, which saved them, though it helped his ruin." (History of his own time, Vol. III., Bk. IV., p. 21.)

The Earl continued with the fleet, and sailed round to Campbeltown, where he issued his manifesto, drawn up in Holland. To rouse his kinsmen thoroughly, he also resorted to the Fiery Cross. Macaulay says

"Zealous as Argyle was for what he considered pure religion, he did not scruple to practise one rite, half popish half pagan. The mysterious cross of yew, first set on fire, and then quenched in the blood of a goat, was sent forth to summon all the Campbells from sixteen to sixty." (His. of England, Vol. I., chap. v., p. 552.)

After considerable delay at Campbeltown, waiting for reinforcements, news at last came that Sir Duncan Campbell of Auchinbreck's (who resided then at the Castle of Carnasary) men were ready. The Earl ordered him to march them to Tarbert. Thither the Earl came with three companies from Islay, three companies from Kintyre, and a troop of horse under Col. Rumbold.

At Tarbert about a thousand men, chiefly from Sir Duncan, joined the Earl. Here he marshalled his little army into three regiments. The whole force assembled, numbering about eighteen hundred men, and Sir Duncan Campbell, John Ayloffe, and Robert Elphinstone of Lapness, were made Colonels. Alex. Campbell of Barbreck, James Henderson, John Fullarton and John Campbell, Majors. Inferior officers were also appointed, and the whole put into the best possible order.

Here the rivalry which had begun in Holland, and continued during the whole course of the expedition, became more violent than ever. The great question was, whether the Highlands or the Lowlands was to be the seat of war. The Earl was desirous to re-establish his authority in his own country, drive out the Marquis of Athole, who was then made Lord Lieutenant of the shire of Argyle, and get possession of his family seat at Inveraray, then he might expect many hesitants to flock to his standard, and with such a force he would be able to defend that rough country against superior forces, and secure an excellent base for offensive operations. Sir Patrick Hume of Polwart, and Sir John Cochrane of Ochiltree, the leaders of the Lowland faction, were determined to divide the forces, especially the latter, who exclaimed that if nobody else would go to Ayrshire, he would go alone with a cornfork. (Wodrow's Hist., Bk. III. c. IX.

The Lowland faction prevailed. The forces were conveyed from Tarbert to the Island of Bute. The van of the army, under the command of Sir John Cochrane, with Colonel Elphinstone and Major Fullarton, was sent to the Lowlands, but finding the English frigates cruising on the Ayrshire coast, they did not attempt landing there, but sailed up the Clyde to Greenock, where they had a skirmish with a band of the Royal Militia, which they put to flight, but they could not persuade the inhabitants to revolt. All they secured was forty bolls of meal, with which they returned, and rejoined the Earl in the Island of Bute.

The Earl renewed his proposal to make an attempt on Inveraray, but he was stoutly opposed. The seamen sided with Hume and Cochrane, but the Highlanders were absolutely at the command of Maccailean-more. There were reasons to fear that the two parties would come to blows and the dread of the consequences inclined the leaders to compromise the matter.

The Castle of Eilean Dearg (the subject of this note) situated at the mouth of Lochruel, was chosen to be the chief place of arms, and thither their fleet sailed. The military stores and provisions were disembarked there. The squadron was moored on the east side of the island, where it was protected by rocks and shallows, and a battery was planted on the other side, mounting several cannons. While this was being accomplished, the land forces, including Rumbold's troops, were transported across the Kyles of Bute to Cowal, and made their way up Lochruel side, till they arrived opposite the Castle of Eilean Dearg.

The Earl, having resolved to be free, once for all, from the cabals of his compatriots, determined to make a descent on Inveraray. The number who volunteered to accompany him was about 1200, the remainder stayed behind at the Castle with the fleet. He divided his volunteers into two battalions, one of which was under himself, and the other he gave in charge to Colonel Rumbold, and sent him to guard a pass in which the Marquis of Athole might attack him. (Wod. Hist., Bk III., Chap. ix.) I have generally followed Mr Wodrow's narrative of this affair, but differ from him on this point. Instead of sending Colonel Rumbold to *guard* a pass, it ought to have been said that he was sent to *clear* a pass, that lay between Eilean Dearg and Inveraray, through which the Earl and his army had to march. If Col. Rumbold was merely to guard the pass, he would require to remain there until the Earl and his battalion got safe through, but, instead of that, Colonel Rumbold cleared the pass, pushed forward and took the castle of Ardkinglass before the Earl arrived there. The tradition of the district bears me out in this idea. The pass in question is a deep water course on the farm of Kilbridemore in Glendaruel, on the way leading to Inveraray, called Sloc-na-nuice. At the head of this pass the Marquis of Athole had an army encamped to intercept the Earl. There is a mound of earth raised on the spot which is yet called Druimnan-Atholach. The lower end of the pass, called Tighnancuiltean, was tenanted by Maolmoire MacNeacail, the great-great-grandfather of Mr Donald M'Nicol, who now farms the same lands. It is said that Maolmoire rendered eminent assistance to Colonel Rumbold in routing the Atholians.

The natives of Glendaruel seem to have followed the Earl's army. There is a tradition in our family, that my great-great-grandfather, James Brown, who resided at Tomlia, fought with the Earl's army at Lochfine-head, and that while the battle was going on, his wife at home resorted to *sliansenrachd*—a pagan art of divining or foretelling, through the shoulderblade of a sheep, the result of the battle.

The Earl, following in the wake of Rumbold, was informed of Maolmoire's bravery, and accosted him in Gaelic   "Ciod a bheir mi dhuit airson do thapachd?"

Maolmoire replied   "Tighnancuiltean gu brath, gu brath."

Argyle was rather taken aback at the demand, and gruffly said   "A bhodaich, nach fhoghnadh e dhuit ri d'bheo, ri d'bheo."

I presume Maolmoire had to be content with a life time of it (if he got that same) as none of his descendants seem to have been called Barons or Bonnet-lairds.

I have already mentioned that Colonel Rumbold had taken the Castle of Ardkinglass. The Marquis of Athole made an attempt to retake it, but Argyle having now arrived, the Marquis, finding his mistake, made a halt at the head of Lochfine. Argyle, with five companies of foot, and two of horse, at once went in person, and attacked the enemy and put t'em to flight. After this skirmish Argyle returned to Ardkinglass, and intended next day to march on Inveraray. But, unhappily, news came that the English men-of-war were forcing their way through the Kyles of Bute, and that some of the gentlemen who would not accompany him to Inveraray, and who had differed from him all along, now threatened to quit all and go to the Lowlands. The Earl was, therefore, obliged to return at once to Eilean Dearg, which he did with three companies of foot, ordering the rest of his army, under Colonel Rumbold and Sir Duncan Campbell, to meet him at the Kirk of Glendaruel. In passing, I may mention that Sir Duncan and his forefathers were not strangers in Glendaruel, being proprietors there, and deriving their title from a farm in that district. They also seem to have taken an interest in its early ecclesiastical affairs. Sir Dugald Campbell, the first baronet of this family, was knighted by King James the Sixth, and got a charter under the Great Seal in 1617, of certain lands in Bute. He was again, by King Charles the first, created a baronet of Nova Scotia, by royal patent, to himself and his male heirs, dated 28th March, 1628. This Sir Dugald has his crest and initials, with date 1610 engraved in relief on a corner-stone of the parish church of Kilmodan, in Glendaruel. (See Douglass' Baronage.)

To return, when the Earl came to Eilean Dearg, he resolved to equip his flotilla, which lay there, and attack the English frigates. It consisted of three ships, brought from Holland, four prizes caught at sea, and thirty large cowans, or fishing boats, with a thousand men he had at his command. But another mutiny was raised among the seamen, by those who still embarrassed him, so that his plan had to be abandoned, and he himself forced into the measures of those who were resolved at all hazards to be off to the Lowlands.

All now was confusion and dismay. The provisions had been mismanaged, and there was no longer food for the forces. The Highlanders, consequently, deserted in hundreds. The fleet being hemmed in by the royal frigates, an escape by sea was impossible. He had no alternative but to face a round about overland march. Before starting, he left the keeping of the castle to Colonel Robert Elphinstone of Lapness, with one hundred and fifty men, with orders, if he was not able to hold out, to blow up the magazine, and either run the ships ashore, or sink them.

The Earl then, with the fragment of the army which had not deserted, retraced his movements to the Kirk of Glendaruel, already agreed upon and had a council of war there with Sir Duncan and Colonel Rumbold. Before proceeding to the Lowlands, they resolved to go in pursuit of the Marquis of Athole, which they did for several days, but to no purpose, as he constantly fled before them.

He then marched for the Lowlands towards the shores of Lochlong,
passed that arm of the Clyde in boats by night (probably at Ardentinny)
went round the Gareloch, and across the river Leven. On the way thither,
he had several skirmishes with bands of militia, which he always put to
flight. But on arriving at Dunbarton, he found a strong body of regular
and irregular troops, prepared to encounter him. He was for giving them
battle, but Hume and his party declared that to engage the enemy would
be sheer madness, that the best course was to remain quiet till night, and
then give the enemy the slip. Since it was overruled not to fight, he was
obliged to retreat. There was a plausible possibility that, by decamping
secretly, and hastening all night across the moor, they might gain many
miles on the enemy before the morning, and might reach Glasgow without further trouble. The watch fires were left burning, and the march
began, but now came the climax of their disasters. The guides mistook
the way across the moor, and led the troops into boggy ground. Military
order could not be preserved. Every sight and sound were thought to
indicate the approach of the pursuers. The army became a disorderly
mob, and many ran away, under cover of the night. At daybreak, only
five hundred fugitives, wearied and dispirited, assembled at Kilpatrick.

All thoughts of prosecuting the war was now at an end. The leaders
fled, for safety, in different directions. Argyle crossed the Clyde near
Kilpatrick, assumed the dress of a peasant, and feigned to be the guide
of his fast friend Major Fullarton. They journeyed together towards
Inchinnan, to a ford where the streams of the Black and White Carts
meet, which was guarded by a band of militia. Questions were asked,
and the Earl was suspected and seized. He broke loose from his captors,
sprang into the water, and stood at bay for a short time against five
assailants, but, having no arms but his pocket pistols, and they being
wet in consequence of the plunge, they would not go off. He was at last
struck down with a broad sword, secured, taken to Edinburgh, and after
suffering great indignities, was beheaded, not for the offence of this re-
bellion, but pursuant to the mock trial, and sentence pronounced on him
in 1681.

The sequel of the story about the castle of Eilean Dearg has now
to be told. I have already observed that the keeping of the castle
was given to Colonel Elphinstone of Lapness ; that he was instructed, if
not able to hold out, to blow up the magazines and sink the ships.
Two days after the Earl and his forces had departed, the English
frigates came in sight of the castle. The governor and his garrison
became panic-struck, landed, and betook themselves for safety among
the rocks and woods of Portaneilean, without firing a shot. The ships
he entirely neglected, but previous to their flight, he laid a train of powder to blow up the magazine. To crown his incapacity for such a charge,

he left behind him the few prisoners taken in the Orkneys, who, being at liberty, immediately acquainted the commanders of the English frigates, (who came ashore in longboats) where the train of powder lay ; which they removed. They then gutted the castle of its contents, sapped its foundations, blew it up, left it a complete wreck, and then seized the ships.

APPENDIX H.

The editor of the "Annals of the Four Masters" is very confident on this point. He says, " The Danish forces, in four great bodies, commanded by Godfrey, son of Ivar, Reginald, Otter and Gragaban, after a fierce battle, were defeated with a great slaughter, and Otter, with many of his chiefs, were slain." (Ann. of the Four Masters, 4to ed. f.n., Dub. 1846). Unfortunately, the editor has not given his authority for this assertion, and certainly it is not in the text. It might be asked if each of the four divisions were severally led as *alleged*, by Reginald and Godfrey, the sons of Ivar, and the two jarls, *Otter* and *Gragaban*. What became of the division, commanded by the *young lords*, as all the copies of the Annals of Ulster assert that the young lords, or chieftains, commanded the *third division*. Our historians seem to have been misled by a quotation in Simeon of Durham's " Life of Saint Cuthbert," which mentions "Otter, Comus and Osval Cracaba as being with Reginald rex, at the taking and pillage of Dublin about the year 912." (Chal. Caledonia.) But strange to say, the Irish Annalists, who ought to be best informed about local affairs, are silent on this subject. I may here quote what Pinkerton says regarding this annalist:—" Simeon's work often errs against Chronology, and seems a late forgery." (Enq., Vol. II., p. 182. f.n.)

The name Oitir is purely a Gaelic word, and is thus defined in M'Leod and Dewar's Gaelic Dictionary : "Oitir, a bank, or ridge of the sea, a shoal or shallow, a low promontory jutting out into the sea." The late Professor M'Lauchlan of Aberdeen, in his beautiful translation of Homer's Iliad, applies the term in the same sense:—

> " Dh'eirich Nestor mannta min
> Righ Philos nan *oitir ban*."

which is rendered in the English versions—Nestor of the *sandy realms*, and also of the *sandy shores*.

The great sandbank or Oitir in Cowal juts about a mile into the sea rather more than half way across Lochfine—and what is dry of it is not much broader than an ordinary country road. It is so peculiar that the district is named after it—AN OITIR. The Danish invaders could not have chosen a more suitable place to land their hosts, as this long ridge, which is dry at half tide, forms an excellent breakwater, on which their whole fleet could run how on, on the lee side, where they could easily disembark.

APPENDIX I.

On the battle-field at Garvie were erected two cairns, a large and a small one, regarding which the ecclesiastical statistics of the parish say —" There are two tumuli, supposed to have been raised by the Norwegians, but have not yet been opened, (in 1790-1.)" Unfortunately, both are now wholly removed, and all that can indicate where they were are their sites marked on the Survey Maps.

The *cairabeg* was merely a small mound of earth. On its removal by Mr Archibald Currie, tenant of Garvie, about 65 years ago, (I was informed by his daughter, the late Mrs Cameron of Ardaphubuil), that two stone coffins were found on the top of it. The *cairamore*, on the other hand, when entire, was an immense heap of waterworn stones, apparently taken from the bed of the Garbh-amhain, which passed its base. It covered the top of a gravelly knoll in the middle of the field, under the present house of Garvie, and was of a circular form, surrounded by an earthen sunk fence. The first encroachment on this sacred pile was made by Mr Currie, who took a great quantity of stones from the top of it to build a wall to the south of it, about half a mile long, and five feet high, and which remains there yet. Mr Walter Black, Mr Currie's successor, made a breach on the south-west side for building stones, and his servants, Donald Black and Stephen Anderson, found in its margin a stone coffin, about two feet long, and covered with a large flag, containing two large human thigh bones. Mr Cunningham of Craigends, who succeeded Mr Black, also removed a great quantity of stones, to build dykes, and the present farm steading of Garvie. The next removal of stones was for banking the river, under Kilbridemore. Donald Black and my (late) father, James Brown, having contracted to quarry stones for the embankment, were allowed to take what they required out of Cairnmore, as the only convenient rock was unsuitable for the purpose. On making a breach on its west side, they found it a heap of clean stones, ready for use. The most curious thing they met with was a side stone wall, or sunk fence, about three or four feet high, facing northwards, and running along the bottom of the cairn, from west to east, through the centre. North of the wall several stone coffins were afterwards found, containing stone jars, and others only black greasy mould or ashes. The final clearing of the cairn was made by Mr Gordon, factor, Glendaruel, after he went to reside in Garvie.

Being often about this cairn during my school days, and afterwards being informed of the discoveries made in it from time to time, I was curious to know about its contents, size, and final clearance, and therefore made enquiry at Mr Gordon, who kindly gave me a note, with the following information, of the share he had in its removal:

"Auchaneilat, 13th May, 1863.

Dear Sir,

The area covered by Cairnmore was about 1398 yards. I took 290 carts of stones out of it, for brow-banking the river at Kilbridemore before I went to reside at Garvie.

When I commenced to clear it entirely away, there was still a great quantity of stones in it ; but as they were not all taken away at once, I did not keep a note of the number of carts. The average depth of gravelly clay taken off the knoll under the cairn was about five feet, and the stones and gravel were chiefly taken to drain and fill up an old course of the river, which ran diagonally into one of the parks south-west of it.

In the removal of the cairn, several stone coffins were found on the north-east side of it. In one I found a stone jar containing ashes (the jar was unfortunately broken). The other coffins were empty, perhaps their contents might have been taken away by those who preceded me in the removal of stones, as several of the coffins were laid bare. I expected to find a coffin in the centre of the cairn, but found none.

I spent a part of three winters in its removal.

I am, dear Sir,

Yours very truly,

ALEX. GORDON."

It is surmised that the Cairnmore had been erected by the Scots after the battle, and that the wall built through the centre of it would be to separate their ashes from that of the Lochannaich. This is obvious, for all the coffins were on the north-east side or face of the wall, none being found at the back of it, except the stone coffin (already referred to) found in the margin, containing bones, and which was of a much later date. It also appears that it was only the chieftains who fell in battle, who were interred there. If the cairn had been erected over a chief, his grave would naturally be placed in the centre of it, but, Mr Gordon says he expected to find a stone coffin there, but found none. This idea is in keeping with the " Annals of Ulster," which says " neither their king nor any maormor fell."

APPENDIX J.

Running parallel to Acha-ghlinn-a-chatha, on the south side, is a deep ravine, the course of a mountain stream. At a narrow neck of it a

F

Dane, when hotly pursued. is said to have leapt across which place is yet called *Leam-an-Lochan....ich*, or the Dane's leap.

There are also on the battlefield two stones called *Leac....a-...a-sle..ph*, or the flag stones of spears, the faces of which are respectively drilled with seventeen and twenty-three holes or cups. Various conjectures are entertained as to the name and puncturing. One is. that the stones, when on end. were *cuspairean*, or butts, at which the native heroes practiced spearmanship. Mr Duncan Whyte, an intelligent member of the Cowal Society, was the first who told me of these stones. He informs me that punctured stones are found in many parts of the country, and that each cup or hole is said to indicate the death of a hero who fell in battle.

APPENDIX K.

The Rev. Alexander M'Farlane, in the old Ecc. Statistics of the parish of Kilfinan, among other things, says :—" The most remarkable antiquities in this parish are Cairns, Duns and Borradhs. The cairns are large piles of stones heaped together. where battles are supposed to have been fought, and where heroes fell and were buried. The Duns are a row of large stones put together, generally in a circular form, on the tops of conspicuous hills. In this parish many of these are to be seen. And the Borradh is also a pile of stones, but differs from the cairns in many respects, viz.. in external figure, being oblong in internal construction, and in its size and design. There are two vestiges of them in this parish. which, though they are now dilapidated for building houses and walls, yet so much remains of each as to show distinctly what they once were. One of them is a mile-and-a-half north of the parish church. on the top of an eminence. This immense pile of stones, which was till last summer (1794), forty yards long, of considerable breadth, and amazing depth. At the bottom, from the one end to the other, there were a number of small apartments or cells, end to end, made up of flags ; each cell was about six feet long, four feet broad, and five feet high." (Vol. XIV.. pp. 256-71.) Mr M'F. starts various conjectures about the use of the cells or stone coffins, some of which are rather fanciful. Among others (which seems to have been their real use). he says : - " Some think they were burying places for the ashes of heroes and great warriors, and human bones have been often found in them." (Ibid.)

These Cairns, Duns and Borradhs. and also mounds of earth where human remains were found, are yet looked upon as the abodes of ghosts and fairies. What native of Oitir is not familiar with the enchanted

Bar-ile, Bar-oile Bar-lagain

Duin-acha-le-ghadain

Agus Clabain Bhar-longairt

Besides these and many others, I was informed by my friend Mr Arch. Crawford, a native of Oitir, that when the present tenement of Largiemore was being built, on clearing the foundation, a number of stone coffins were found, so that the natives for a long time dreaded to pass that place at night. On the Maps of the recent Survey are marked several cairns in the district, some of them are of considerable dimensions. There are also traditional stories in the district of battles, and single combats, having taken place there. One of them is told of a Manx hero, who, when his followers were routed, defended himself against a rock, on which, it is said, he left the print of his back—the rock is still called Sgeir-a-Mhannanich. It might be asked what were Manxmen doing in Oitir? But it is a curious coincidence that the Isle of Man was a place of resort, if not actually possessed by this Danish dynasty at this particular time. Four years previous to the invasion, we find Reginald fighting a naval battle there, with another of the same race. " Anno 914—Acris pugna navalis propi Manaim Insulam, inter Baredum et Reginaldum O'Hivar Danos, commissum est, in qua Reginaldus, Baredo suis occissis, victoriam reportavit." (Johnstone's Antiq., Celto-Normanica, p. 77) It is possible the fleet by which Reginald invaded Cowal might have partly been recruited at the Isle of Man.

APPENDIX L.

The conflict at Srath-nan-Lochannaich, though severe, was not considered of so much moment as the great battle at Garvie. At Srath-nan-Lochannach, it is said the Danes kept sentry on a piece of level ground (now planted) on the hill-side west of the battle-field, and there are shewn two places on the east of the field, where their dead were buried, but on neither of these spots are there any standing stones, cists or cairns. The Rev. John M'Kinnon, (who was a stranger in the place) does not specify the particular place of battle which gave the glen its name, but from his reference to the " two tumuli, supposed to have been raised by the Norwegians, but still unopened," we may safely infer he meant Garvie. Mr John M'Kellar, farmer, Strondaven, father of the late Captain M'Kellar, of Sydney, and grandfather of M'Kinlay, the eminent Australian explorer, who was born in the year 1734, and died in 1830. He was thus fifty-six years old when the Ecc. Stat. were written. Mr M'K. was well educated, and full of the tradition of the district, and always said (to some yet living) that the great battle, which gave the glen its name, was fought at Garvie, where the cairns were erected.

APPENDIX M.

In the discussion that followed the reading of this Essay, it was questioned whether the inhabitants of Cowal had taken part in this memorable engagement, and even if the district had been inhabited at that remote period. If either had been the case, (however much this narrative might concern others, it would be shorn of its interest to the Cowal Society. There is abundant evidence to show, that Cowal had been inhabited long prior to this event, and I presume we may safely infer that the natives of Cowal had their share in the victory achieved. Indeed, a tradition of the district is, that the victory was won by the natives themselves, with the help of the Araghalaich, or the people of Argyle proper.

A short sketch of this district and people prior to this invasion may, perhaps, satisfy those who are sceptical on this point.

The first people, we learn, who inhabited this district (about the middle of the second century of the Christian era) were called Attacoti. This tribe is said to have occupied the whole country, from Lochfine on the west, to the river of Leven on the east, comprehending the whole of Cowal and the greater part of Dumbartonshire. (Chal. Cal., Vol. I., 64.

But, passing from conjectural annals, to the real history of this people, we have a sure epoch to commence with the arrival of the Scots colony from Dalriada, in the North of Ireland (about the year 495 A.D.) under the leadership of the three sons of Erc.—Loarn, Fergus and Angus. The locality which these originally colonized embraced the greater part of Argyleshire, to which they gave the name Dalriada. This name is said to have been derived from Cairbre-Riada, cousin and general of King Cormac, who reigned over Ireland about the middle of the third century. Cairbre-Riada, having quelled some disturbances between two factions, seized their possessions, which were about thirty miles in extent, and called them *Dalriada*, or the portion of Riada. Hence the name given by his descendants to their colony in Albin.

This territory was divided between the leaders of this colony. The race of Angus occupied the islands of Jura and Islay, their probable stronghold being Dunyveg, or Dunaomhaig, in Islay. The race of Loarn occupied the district of Lorn, their chief stronghold was at Duinolaigh, near Oban. Fergus had a son called Domangart, who had two sons called Comgall and Gabhran. The race of Gabhran inhabited Argyle proper, and Kintyre, their chief stronghold, was on the rocky conical hill north of the Crinan Canal, called Dunatt, and Dunmonaidh, which yet shows the remains of strong fortifications of a primitive type : they had also the castle of Dunaverty in Kintyre. The race of Comgall inhabited the district of Cowal, which was formerly spelled Comgall, Congel, and also Comhghall. Comgall having given his name to this district, doubtless had

his special residence there, which probably was the Castle of Dunoon.
Their original fortresses would thus be Dunad, Dunaverty, Donolly,
Dunoon, and Dunaomhaig.

These were the districts occupied by the descendants of the sons of
Erc. Their influence, both from a religious and political point of view,
extended as a beacon of light among the nations around them, who were
yet groping in gross darkness.

The part played by these colonists has hitherto been described from
extreme points of view. In the earlier histories of Scotland, everything
that was great and good, was ascribed to the Scots of Dalriada. In the
year 843 they are said to have exterminated the Picts, and annexed their
kingdom to their own. On the other hand, from the time that Father
Innes published his Critical Essays (1729), the early deeds of the Scots
of Dalriada in many respects have been denied, and slighted by him
and many others.

The Government publication of the Chronicles of the Picts and Scots,
printed in Edinburgh about seven years ago, places the materials of which
our early history is founded, in the hands of the public. These documents, accompanied by an extensive preface, and a copious index, by the
learned editor, Mr W. F. Skene, put the early history of our country on
a more intelligible footing than any yet attempted.

Mr Skene shews, that, shortly after the Scots of Dalriada had colonized
Argyle, Albuin or present Scotland, had been inhabited by four distinct
nations, viz.—The Irish Scots inhabited Argyle ; the Picts the remainder
of Scotland north of the Clyde and Forth ; the Angles of Bernicia extended their territories on the east from the Humber to the Forth ; and
the Britons extended their kingdom on the west from Wales to the
Clyde.

In giving further particulars regarding the Dalriadic race, for the sake
of connection, it will be necessary to trace the different branches of this
family, as they appeared in *power*, during the era under consideration.

This colony (as we have already seen), came from Ireland about the
year 495 A.D., when Fergus Mor Mac Erc seems to have been chosen king.
He reigned three years, and was succeeded by his brother Angus Mor
Mac Erc, who reigned five years. He was succeeded by Domangort,
son of Fergus, who also reigned five years. This king was the first of
his race, who extended his kingdom beyond the limits of Dalriada, for
Tighernac terms him " Righ Alban." Domangort was succeeded by his
son, Comgall, who reigned twenty-four years, or as others have it, thirty
years. He is also, by the same annalist, styled " Rig Alban." The Duan
Albanach says of him—

          " A xxiiii gun troid
            Do Comgall mac Domhangoirt."

i.e. --" Twenty-four years without a battle.
To Comgall, son of Domangort."

This goes to shew that his title to the extended dominions had not been disputed during his reign. He was succeeded by his brother Gabhran, who is also termed " Ri Alban." After twenty-two years of prosperous reign, he died or was killed in battle, for in the same year in which he died, the Scots of Dalriada were driven out of Pictland by Bruide, son of Maileon, king of the Picts. From that date their designation was changed from that of kings of Alban to that of Dalriada. Gabhran was succeeded by Conall, the son of Comgall. In the third year of his reign St Columba came to Britain, and appeared before King Conall. In the thirteenth year of his reign, he gave the island of Iona to St. Columba Adomnan and Tighernac. The Duan Albanach says of him :

" Tri bliadhna fo cuig gan roinn,
Ba ri Connall mac Comhghoill."

i.e.- Three years five times, without interruption, was King Conall, son of Comgall. His son Duncan attempted to succeed him as King of Dalriada, but his right was disputed by his cousin Aedan, the son of Gabhran,—when a battle ensued, in which Duncan and many of his followers were slain. "Cath Delgon a Cindtire in quo Donchadh mac Connaill mic Comgaill acus alii de sociis filiorum Garbhain ceciderunt." (Tighernac). Aedan having thus triumphed over his rival, succeeded Connall, and was solemnly crowned by St. Columba. He reigned 24 years, during which time he fought other four battles the battle of Manann, in 582 or 583,—the battle of Leithrig in 590 that of Circhind in 596, lastly, with Ethelfrid, King of Bernicia, in 600, against whom he appears to have led an army of Scots and Britons into Northumbria, and was there defeated "Bellum Saxonum in quo victus est Aedan." (Ann. Ulst.) Aedan died in the year 606, and was succeeded by his son Eocha Buidhe. The Albanic Duan says of him,

" Ten years and seven, a glorious career
In the sovereignty Ethach Buidhe."

Eocha Buidhe was succeeded by his son Conad Cerr (Kenneth sinister who only reigned three months, when he was slain in battle by Maileaich mac Seannail, king of the Picts.

Conad Cerr was succeeded by his son. Fearchair, who reigned sixteen years, during which, nothing of any consequence is said regarding him. Ferchar was succeeded by Donnall Bree mac Eocha Buidhe, who reigned fourteen years. In the last year of his reign (642) Domnal Bree fought a battle at Sraith Cairinn, with Hoan, King of the Britons of Strath Clyde, and was slain there.

For upwards of forty years after the death of Donnal Bree, Dalriada seems to have been subject to the Britons of Strath-Clyde, and the Angles of Bernicia. During this subjugation, the following kings nominally reigned over Dalriada (642 to 685)

Comal Crandomna and Dunchad mac Daban } together,	- - - -	10 years
Domnal Donn, - - - - - - - - -		13 „
Mailduin mac Comall, - - - - - - -		17 „
Ferchar fada, during the early part of his reign,	- -	3 „

43 years

For the first fifteen years of this era, the Scots were subject to the Britons. At the end of which (655) Oswy, King of the Angles, overcame Penda, and his allies, in a great battle near Falkirk. By this defeat the Britons seem to have fallen into the power of Oswy, and the Scots of Dalriada, who were subject to the former, appear to have shared the same fate. Three years after this victory, Oswy subdued the southern parts of Pictland, and kept possession of it till his death in 670, when he was succeeded by his son Eegfrid.

Prior to this double conquest, the Kings of Dalriada (with the exception of Angus Mor Mac Erc) were all of the race of Fergus, that is to say, either of that of Comgall or Gabhran, but, during the conquest, Ferchar fada, who was head of the rival house of Loarn, appears to have taken the lead in recovering the independence of the Scots. He died in 697, after a reign of twenty-one years, being the first three years subject to the Angles, the other eighteen years free.

Shortly after the accession of Eegfrid, both the Scots and Picts made strong attempts to throw off the yoke of the Angles. In 681 the "Annals of Ulster" records the siege of Dunfother ; in 683 the siege of Duinatt and Dunduirn. Dunfother and Dunduirn were the chief seats of two of the seven provinces of the Picts ; and Dunatt was the central capital of Dalriada. Eegfrid finding this general revolt, in 685 led his army to the southern parts of Pictland. Having been led by a feigned flight into the mountains of Forfarshire "augustias inaccessorum montium" (Bede), he was then, on the 15th day before the kalends of June, waylaid and slain, and his whole army cut to pieces by Brude M'Bile, king of Fortren. The Scots and Picts took advantage of this victory, for, in the same year the Angles seem to have burnt, or been burnt out, of two of their acquired strongholds, viz., Tula-aman, a stronghold on the Tay, near Scone ; and Duinollaigh, the stronghold of the house of Loarn, " Combussit Tula-aman (et Duinollaig." (Ann. Ulst.) The Angles now appear to have been completely crushed. The venerable Bede, writing about the disasters of Ecgfrid and his army, says "From this time the hopes and strength of the English crown began to waver and retrograde." (B. IV. c. 26.) And forty-six years after this event (731) this venerable author, with much satisfaction, says—"The Scots that inhabit Britain (Dalriada), satisfied with their own territories, meditate no hostilities against the nations of the Angles." (B. V. c. 23.)

But, to return to the state of affairs in Dalriada. After the Scots had gained their independence, Ferchar fada, having died in 697, left two sons, Ainbhceallach and Selbhach; the former succeeded his father, and reigned only one year, when it appears his brother, dispossessed him. The "Annals of Ulster" says, "in 698 Dunolly was burnt, and Ainbhceallach, the son of Ferchar, was expelled the kingdom and taken bound to Ireland. "Combustio Duinonlaigh expulsio Ainfceallach filii Ferchir de regno et vinctus ad Hiberniam vehitor." (Ann. Ulst.)

For thirty years afterwards, Selbhach ruled Dalriada with a high hand, and also fought several battles with the Britons. At first he seems to have met some resistance from his brother's sympathisers, which he retaliated. For three years after his brother's expulsion (701) he destroyed Dunolly. "Destructio, Duinonlaigh apud Sealbach." (Ann. Ulst.)

In 704, we learn that the Dalriadans were slaughtered at a place called Valle Limnae "Strages Dalriati in Valle Limnae," (Ann. Ulst) which I presume was the Vale of Leven. Not many years afterwards, several engagements took place between the Scots of Dalriada and the Britons of Strath Clyde, whose stronghold was Ailcluaith or Dumbarton Castle, when the tables were turned against the Britons. In 710 a battle took place between the race of Comgall, that is, the inhabitants of Cowal, and the Picts, when two of the sons of Nechtan, the son of Doirgarto were slain. "Imbairece apud genus Comgaill ubi duo filii Nechtan meic Doirgarto jugulati sunt." (Ann. Ulst.

In 711 the Britons and Dalriadans fought a battle at Loirg-Eclat, where the Britons were conquered. "Congressio Brittonum et Dalriadha for Loirg-Eclat ubi Britones devicti." (Ann. Ulst.)

In 712 Selbhach besieged the castle of Dunaverty. "Absessio Aberto apud Selbacum." (Ann. Ulst.) And in the same year Tairpirt Boetter, the other stronghold of the race of Gabhran in Kintyre was burnt. —"Combustio Tairpirt Boetter." (Ann. Ulst.) I presume this was the ancient royal castle of Tarbert, Lochfine, which was of so much importance in after years, both to Kings Edward I. and Robert Bruce.

In 717 an engagement took place between the Scots and the Britons, at a place called Minvirce, where the Britons were overcome.—"Congressio Dalriati acus Britonum in lapide qui vocatur Minvirce et Britonis devicti sunt." (Ann. Ulst.) In 719 Ainbhceallach, after being in exile for twenty-one years, returns from Ireland apparently with the object of recovering his lawful kingdom of Dalriada, and has a pitched battle with his brother Selbhach at a place called Finnghlinne, where Ainbhceallach was slain. "Cath Finnglinne itir da meic Fearchair fota in qui Ainbhceallach jugulatus est die quinte ferie 11 Sep." (Tigherme.) In the following month of the same year, a naval battle was fought at Ardeaneshie, between Dunchadbeee *rex Ciantire* (who was of the race of Gabhran) and Selbhach, when Dunchadh was defeated. In 728 a battle was fought at Ross-feochan between Selbhach and Eachdach, the grandson of Domnall Brec, the result is not given.

In 730 Selbhach mac Ferchair, after having ruled Dalriada for thirty-two years, died. "Selbhach mac Fercair Mortuus est." (Ann. Ulst.) In 731 Selbhach's footsteps were followed by his son Donald, whose first act was to burn the castle of Tarbert. "Combustio Tairpirt Boittir apud Dungal." (Ann. Ulst.) In the same year a battle was fought between the Scots and Picts at Murbulg, in Dalriada, where the Picts were defeated --" Cath itir Cruithnin acus Dalriada in Murbulg ubi Cruithnin devicti." (Tighernac)

In 733 Donald disgraced himself by plundering religious houses in the neighbouring islands. " Dungal mac Selbaich dehoneravit," &c. (Ann. Ulst.) In the same year Muredac mac Ainbhceallach, the lineal descendant of Ferchar fada *assumed* the kingdom. Muredac mac Ainfceillach regnum generis Loairnd assumit." (Ann. Ulst.)

In 736, Angus, the son of Fergus, King of the Picts, laid waste the kingdom of Dalriada, seized Dunat, burnt Creie, and put Dungall and Ferdach, the two sons of Selbhach, in chains. No sooner were the sons of Selbhach overcome, than their cousin Talorgan, son of Ainbhceallach, and grandson of Ferchar fada tries his fortune in battle with the Picts, near Falkirk, where he and many of his followers were slain.

741. The battle of Drumcathmail, between the Picts and Dalriads, where the latter were beaten by Oengus mac Ferguso, king of the Picts.

For upwards of one hundred years after this event, there is the greatest confusion in the history of the Dalriadic kings. On the one hand, the Gaelic lists of Flann Mainistreach, and the Duan Albanach of the eleventh century, vary very much from the Latin lists of a later date. The learned editor of the chronicles sympathises with the former, and characterises the Latin lists as " the later forms of Scottish fable." He further says " The compilers of the Latin list suppressed the conquest of Dalriada by the Picts, and the century of the Pictish rule in that kingdom, by placing the reigns of the last four kings a century later, and interpolating kings before them to fill up the vacant period." (Skene's Pref. C. VI., p. 134.)

After carefully reading Mr Skene's great work, I humbly think, that his strictures on the Latin lists are far too sweeping.

The following are Mr Skene's chronological tables of the Dalriadic kings of the Gaelic and Latin lists, from Ferchar fada to Kenneth M'Alpin.

GAELIC LISTS.	Reign	Died	LATIN LISTS.	Reign
Ferchar Fada, - - -	21		Ferchar Longus, - - - -	21
Eocho Riananihail, - -	2		Eochal habens curvum nasum	3
Ainbhceallach mac Ferchar	1		Ainchellac fil Ferchar, - -	1
Selbach mac Ferchar, -		741	ob. Ewen filius Ferchar longi	13
Eochaig Angbaidh, - -		744	.. Murechat fil. Ainchellac	3
THIRTEEN KINGS, 743-879				
Dungal mac Selbaig, -	7	747	.. Ewen fil. Murechat, - - -	3
Alpin mac Echach, - -	4			
Muredac na Daite, - -	3			
Aed Aereatach, - - -	30	777	.. Edalbus fil. Eochal, - -	30
Fergus, - - - - - -		781	.. Fergus fil. Hedalbi, - -	3
Eochoid, - - - - -				
Donnall mac Custantin,	24	804	.. Selvach fil. Eogan, - -	24
Connal Caemh, - - -	2			
Conal his brother, - -	4	834	.. Eochal venenosus, filius Hedalbi, - - - -	30
Custantin mac Fergusa,	9			
Aengus mac Fergusa, -	9	841	.. Dunegal filius Selvach, -	7
Aed mac Boanta, - -	4			
Eoganan mac Aengusa,	13	843	.. Alpin fil. Eochal, - - -	3
Cinaed mac Alpin, - -	30	858	.. Cinaed fil. Alpin, - - -	16

In glancing across the two lists, we find them to agree within a year of each other, as to the time Ferchar fada and his two successors reigned, after that they materially disagree. Let us first examine the GAELIC LISTS.—After Ainbhceallach, Selbhach, his brother, is given without the length of time he reigned, but, the Irish annals show that he ruled from 698 to 730. Eachaig Angbaidh is also without a date. After 743, Dungal mac Selbaig is made to reign for seven years, whereas the Irish annals show that he succeeded his father in 731. Alpin mac Echach succeeds Dungal, reigns four years, and is made contemporary with Alpin, the father of Kenneth of the Latin lists. It is very probable that the first Alpin of the Gaelic lists has no claim or title to rank among the kings of Dalriada, but is that Alpin whom Tighernac refers to in the year 728, *Cath Monaigh Craebi itir Picardachibh fein, i.- Aengus meas Alpine issiot tar an cath neas ro mebaigh ria n-Aengus.*" "The battle of Monaigh Craebi between *the Picardich themselves, Alpin* and Angus fought the battle, and the victory was with Angus." Then follow Muredac na Daiti, Aed Aireatach, and Fergus, whose names correspond to those of the Latin lists. The years **Fergus** reigned are left blank, so are those of Eochoid. Donald mac Custantin, a Pict, reigned twenty-

four years. Conall Caemh, and Conall his brother, (or as the Duan Al-
banach has it, another Conall), reigned respectively two and four years.
They appear to have been of the Dalriadic race of Gabhran. The
"Annals of Ulster" mentions that, in 789 a battle took place between
Constantin, king of the Picts, and Conall mac Taidg, when the latter
was overcome, and that in 807 Conall mac Taidg was slaughtered by
Conal, son of Aedan in Kintyre. "Jugulatio Conall mac Taidg o'Conall
meic Aedain i Cuinntire." (Ann. Ulst.) Then follow Constantin mac
Fergusa and Aengus mac Fergusa, both Picts, who reigned respectively
nine years. Aed mac Boanta succeeds them, and reigned four years. He
is said to have been King of Dalriada. After him Eoganan mac Aengusa,
a Pict, reigned thirteen years, and lastly Cinaed mac Alpin, is said to
have reigned thirty years. Let us now examine the

LATIN LISTS. The Latin lists do not give the era in which
Ferchar fada and his two successors flourished, they merely mention the
number of years each reigned, but we learn from the "Annals of Ulster"
that Ferchar fada died in 697, and both lists agree that he reigned 21
years. We have here a proper date to begin with.

Era.		Reign.
676-697	Ferchar longus, - - - - - - - -	21

Eochal habens curvum nasum, son of Domangart, and grandson of Domnall Bree, is said to have reigned three years,
but I think this must be a mistake, as Eochal was of the
race of Gabhran, and the Latin lists down from Ferchar
fada treat of the house of Loarn only. This is clearly
proven in this case by the Irish annals, which shew that
Ainbhceallach, immediately succeeded his father, and left no
interval for Eochal to reign.

698	Arinchellac fil. Ferchar fada, - - - - - -	1
698-730	Selbhach, son of Ferchar fada, - - - - - -	32
731-733	Dungal mac Selbhach, - - - - - - -	3

It may be observed that Selbhach, who was a usurper, and
Dungal, who was a robber, are neither of them acknowledged
in the Latin lists, and the blank from the expulsion of Ainbhceallach in 698, till Muredac, his son, assumit the kingdom
in 733, agrees with the time Selbhach and Donald ruled.

729-741	Ewen filius Ferchar longus	13
741-744	Murechat filius Arinchellac, - - - - - -	3

It would appear that Ewan was appointed Tanister over
the House of Loarn two years before the death of his brother Selbhach, and continued as such for 13 years. From
the "Annals of Ulster," we learn that Muredac, the son of
Ainbhceallach, who was the lineal heir of Ferchar fada,

assumit the kingdom in 733. But according to the law of Tanistry, his uncle Ewan might be considered more fit to rule, and it would be only from the death of Ewan that the reign of Muredac would begin to date.

745-747	Ewen filius Murechat, - - - - - - -	3
748-777	Edalbus filius Eochal, habens curvum nasum, - - -	30

This is evidently a second mistake, founded on the one referred to above. We have seen that Arinchellac directly succeeded Ferchar fada, and left no place for Eochal. Eochal therefore must be a mistranscription, and ought to be Ewen or Eogan. I therefore think that Edalbus is the son of Ewen, the son of Murechat.   •

778-781	Fergus filius Hedalbi, - - - - - - -	3
781-804	Selvach filius Eogan, - - - - - -	24
805-834	Eochal Venenosus filius Hedalbi. - - - -	30
835-841	Dungal filius Selvach, - - - - - - -	7
841-843	Alpin filius Eochal Venenosus. - - -	3
843-858	Kenneth filius Alpin. - - - - -	16

In comparing the merit of both tables, in the Gaelic lists, we find a conglomeration of Dalriadic, Pictish, and non-descript kings raked together, whose dates are generally at variance with contemporary annals. Besides this, there is not a shred of evidence to show that any of the Pictish kings named in the Gaelic lists, occupied Dalriada for a single day after the raid of Angus mac Fergus in 741. It was different with the Kings of Dalriada, for during the very time of their alleged subjugation, we find Aedh or Edalbus, warring with Kenneth, King of the Picts, in the heart of his kingdom. " 768. Bellum i fortrin ittir Aedh acus Cineadh." (Ann. Ulst.)

With regard to the Latin list, with the exception of the few mistakes noticed, which only go to show that they were not *artificially* got up, we have an unbroken line of kings of the house of Loarn, from Ferchar fada to Kenneth M'Alpin. It is true that the four kings preceding Kenneth M'Alpine (although mentioned in various ways in the Latin lists) are not mentioned in the Irish annals, but this is not singular, as the Irish records during *their* reign, give but a very scanty account of Scottish history, they do not even record the union of the Scots and Picts, which was the most important event in Scotland in ancient times. It therefore requires no stretch of imagination to suppose that during these sixty-two years (781-843) the royal race of Loarn reigned quietly in their native district ; however, when the opportunity came, (as I shall shortly mention) a royalist appeared who was equal to the occasion.

The sudden elevation of Kenneth mac Alpin to the united thrones of the

Scots and Picts at Scone in 843, is a puzzle not easily explained by those who maintain that the Dalriadans were, previous to this date, literally crushed—that their proceedings were wholly undeserving of any record and that their affairs bore as little upon the general history of Scotland, as the early Annals of Sussex did upon the general history of England. (Robertson's Gael of Alban, p. 70.) To get rid of this difficulty, it is said that the elevation had taken place in a peaceable way by right of marriage ; but, if such had been the case, it would only go to prove that the union had taken place on equal terms.

A great deal has been written of Kenneth's Pictish connection by the mother side, but this presumption has not been established by any evidence. The cause of the Scottish conquest and elevation of Kenneth must therefore be sought elsewhere. From the chronicles of that period we learn that the marauding Danes were infesting the shores of Pictland, and four years before the conquest Eoganan mac Oengusa and Bran his brother, with their ally Aod mac Boanta, (said to be one of the kings of Dalriada), fought a great battle with the Danes, when the three royalists, with an innumerable number of their followers, were slain " 839. Bellum ri genntib for firu Fortrenn in quo Eoganan mac Oengusa acus Bran mac Oengusa acus Aod mac Boanta et alii (pene) innumerabiles ceciderunt." (Ann. of Ulst.)

This Pictish calamity seems to have been the House of Loarn's opportunity, for Alpin, the father of Kenneth, issued from the seclusion of his principality of Loarn. We learn from the Chronicle of Huntingdon that in the year 834 the Scots encountered the Picts on Easter Day, when many of the Pictish nobles fell, and Alpinus rex Scottorum was victorious ; and that on the 13th day of the kalends of August, in the same year, he was defeated by the Picts, and slain. That his son Kenneth, in the seventh year of his reign, when the Danish pirates occupied the shores, destroyed the Picts with a great slaughter, passed into the remainder of their territories, turned his arms against them, and having slain many, compelled them to fly, and that thus he regained the monarchy of Albania, and first reigns in it over the Scots. That in the twelfth year of his reign he encountered the Picts seven times in one day, and having destroyed many, he confirmed his kingdom, and reigned twenty-eight years."

Mr Skene, from whose preface to the Chronicle I extract this quotation, says " *this seems to be a fragment of true history.*" It is very important to find this admission from such an able critic as Mr Skene, after the many efforts of modern historians to explode the Scottish conquest of the Picts by Kenneth mac Alpin. But, though this fragment of ancient history in the main be true, in comparing it with the most complete Latin chronicles, the Duan Albanach and the Annals of Ulster, it evidently errs against dates. The victory, the defeat, and the death of Alpin, must have taken place between the disaster of the Picts in 839 and their conquest by his son in 843, being the epoch he is said, in the Latin list, to have reigned. It is worthy of remark, that the Pictish Kings from 741 to 839 are regularly recorded in the Irish annals, but after the Danish victory at the latter date, we hear no more of Pictish kings. We afterwards learn of Alpin slaying many *Pictish nobles* in battle, and of his son Kenneth overrunning all Pictland, and destroying many *Picts*, but not a word about *kings*, which fact goes to confirm the idea that it was their disorganized extremity that occasioned their being conquered by an infinitely smaller nation.

Kenneth mac Alpin not only subjugated the Picts, but subjected the whole of modern Scotland under his sway, driving the Angles to the Tweed, and the Britons to the Solway ; and causing the country to be called Scotland The Pictish Chronicle says of him, "Kinadius igitur filius Alpini, primus Scottorum, rexit feliciter istam annis xvi. Pictaviam;" while the " Ann. of Ulster" thus records his death.—"858. Cineath mac Alpin rex Pictorum mortuus est." From 843 to 858, both inclusive, make the sixteen years he is said in the Latin lists to have reigned.

Having got through the tangled maze of Scottish history from 741 to 843, we are now entering on undoubted historic ground. Hitherto I have endeavoured to trace the descendants of Erc, as they severally appeared in power in the four provinces of Dalriada. The house of Loarn was the ruling power, after the release of Dalriada from the yoke of the Angles in 685, till their conquest of the Picts in 843. I shall now name the five Scottish kings that ruled from this era till the Invasion of Cowal in 918.

Donald, who succeeded his brother Kenneth, reigned four years. Constantin, the son of Kenneth, succeeded Donald, and reigned thirty years. During his reign the country had been invaded several times by the Danish kings of Ireland. In 866 these kings laid waste all the Cruithne-tuath (northern Picts) and carried off hostages, while in 870 they besieged and after four months seized Ail-cluaith or Dumbarton Castle. In 875 there was a great slaughter of the Picts by the Danes.

Constantine was succeeded by Aech his brother, who reigned only one or two years, and was slain by his subjects.

Aedh was succeeded by his nephew Donald, son of Constantine, who reigned four years.

And Donald was succeeded by Constantine, the son of Aedh, who, in the eighteenth year of his reign, overcame the Danes in Cowal.

In concluding this note, it must be admitted, that the part played by the race of Comhgall in the affairs of the kingdom of Dalriada, had not been so stirring as either that of Loarn or Gabhran, yet, that race left its footprints on the sands of time, as its founder conferred his name on the district. During Comhgall's long reign of twenty-four or thirty years, the nation enjoyed undisturbed peace—a blessing which would go far to establish law, and propagate the Christian religion not only in Dalriada but over all Scotland, whose king he nominally was, as in the Irish annals he is called " Big Alban."

The possessions of Conal, the son of Comghall, were not so extensive as those of his father. During the reign of his uncle Gabran, who preceded him, the Scots were driven out of the province of the Picts, and afterwards confined within Dalriada proper, until the union of both nations took place. Although Conall's kingdom had thus been circumscribed, he was still a powerful monarch. In the third year of his reign (563) Saint Columba came to Britain, and appeared before the king " Coram Conallo rege filio Comgall;" and in the thirteenth of his reign he gave St Columba a gift of the island of Iona. " XIII. anno, regni sui qui oferavit Insolam Ja Colainneille." (Tighernac)

Duncan, the son of Conal, endeavoured to perpetuate the throne of Dalriada in the house of Comhghall, but his cousin Aedan, the son of Gabhran, disputed his right to reign. The battle of Delgon, in Kintyre, ensued, when Duncan and many of his followers were slain.

From this date, (584 till 642,) we lose sight of the race of Comhgall. After that Conall II., the grandson of Conall I., began to reign. His claims to the kingdom were disputed by Dungall of the race of Loarn, but this contest however, does not appear to have been of long duration, for Conall died in possession of his dominions, after a reign of ten years. Donal-duin, his son, reigned thirteen years, and was succeeded by his brother, Maol-duin, who reigned sixteen years. (Pict. Hist. of Scot.)

I have already observed that these three kings were more nominal than real. During the period of authority ascribed to them, and three years afterwards (642-685) Dalriada appears to have been under the yoke of the Britons and Angles. In the year 685, Ferchar fada, who was then chief of the house of Loarn, appears to have been instrumental in regaining the independence of Dalriada. From this date till the union of the Scots and Picts, which took place in 843, the race of Loarn was the ruling power.

It will be remembered that almost all the conflicts Dalriada had with other nations, occurred eastward of itself, consequently Cowal would necessarily be the debateable ground. Sometimes the inhabitants of Cowal had to maintain their marches alone, as they did in 710, when they overcame the Picts and slew their leaders— the two sons of Nechtan, the son of Doirgarto. But generally speaking, the inhabitants of Dalriada were few when compared with the numerous populations of the nations around them. They therefore had to sink their little feuds and act together when required to cope with these nations, or be swallowed up by them. But the Dalriadans having been able to keep their own ground, whatever success or reverse is ascribed to any branch of the race of Ere is applicable to them all.

I cannot omit that Dalriada was the cradle of the British Monarchy. Before and after the time of the Roman occupation we have had several powerful nations in Britain, including Britons, Picts, Anglo-Saxons, Danes and French Normans. The Britons and Picts have left long lists of kings, many of them of which nothing can be said, sometimes an occasional one of them may come across the page of history, but like the gleam of a meteor, leaving no trace whence he came nor whither he went. The Anglo-Saxons, Danes and Normans, like so many dissolving views, in their turn have displaced one another. But the Scots of Dalriada have an ancient pedigree of Kings which no British nation can boast of. For about 350 years, the royal race was nursed and fostered there from thence transplanted to Scone, and lastly to London, to be crowned on the Scottish Lia Fail, or sacred stone of destiny, in Westminster Abbey.

"Quem Scoti lapidem sanxerunt ponere sedem,
" Regibus inde suis tantum, sed non alienis."

James Storer, Printer, Greenock.

www.ingramcontent.com/pod-product-compliance
Lightning Source LLC
Chambersburg PA
CBHW031804090426
42739CB00008B/1152